The Beta Male Dating Guide:

How to Attract Girls without Trying so Hard

Ben Romero

Copyright © 2019 by Ben Romero

All Rights Reserved

Disclaimer:

No part of this publication may be reproduced or transmitted in any form or by any means, or transmitted electronically without direct written permission in writing from the author.

While all attempts have been made to verify the information provided in this publication, neither the author nor the publisher assumes any responsibility for errors, omissions, or misuse of the subject matter contained in this eBook.

This eBook is for entertainment purposes only, and the views expressed are those of the author alone, and should not be taken as expert instruction. The reader is responsible for their own actions.

Adherence to applicable laws and regulations, including international, federal, state, and local governing professional licensing business practices, advertising, and all other aspects of doing business in the U.S.A, Canada or any other jurisdiction is the sole responsibility of the purchaser or reader.

Contents

Introduction v

Chapter 1: Are you a "Beta" male? 1

    What Exactly does the Term
    "*Beta male*" Mean? 2

Chapter 2: Knowing your Strengths as a
    "*Beta*" Male 6

    Reasons Why Girls Like "Beta" Males 10
    Why Smart Asian Females Tend to Almost
    Always Pick a "*Beta*" over The "*Alpha*" Male 12

Chapter 3: Checking Your Reality Standards 14

    Ways and Options to Meet Other Girls 16
    Setting Up the Right Mindset 19

Chapter 4: The Art of Self-improvement..................... 23

    Having a Goal and a Plan 23
    Dealing with Negative People in Your Life 26

Physical Transformation for increased Confidence................................ 26
Visual Appearance and Confidence Levels 28

Chapter 5: Matching Lifestyles and Compatibility in a Relationship... 30

Signs that You and Your Partner are Compatible....................................... 31

Chapter 6: Improving the Quality of Your Relationship... 36

Chapter 7: Dealing with Anxiety and Rejection.......... 44

Chapter 8: The infamous "*Friend Zone*" 50

Why Does "*The Friend Zone*" Happen? 52
How to Escape the Friend Zone 54
Stand Up for Yourself and Create a Bit of Competition.. 56

Chapter 9: How to be Attractive without Trying Hard..................................... 60

Conclusion 65

Introduction

This book is more of a generalized, unscientific examination of why certain girls like "*Alpha*" males and the other ones are more into so-called "*Betas*"

I do not possess some kind of a high degree in psychology or relationship therapy. Even though I am a professional dating coach now, I was just a <u>normal guy</u> trying to help others achieve what they think is impossible for them by telling them about my past experiences and encounters, mistakes and important lessons that I had to learn the hard way.

I am going to attempt as much as possible to avoid multiple uses of polysyllabic language and speak to you using very simple **easy-to-understand** terminology.

When it comes to dating, women have a variety of tastes. Each has her own feelings about different types of men. Some of them like the highly confident athletic guys with big muscles, others like the more thin and shy type of guys. Is one type superior to the other? Hang tight, we will find out soon!

I'm pretty sure that each one of you is familiar with the term "*Alpha Male*", or have heard it at least once somewhere before. Well, for those who do not know what it means, it is a term used to usually describe a very masculine male person with high levels of confidence and intimidating attitude. Some say that a much bigger percentage of women will always choose the "*Alpha*" over the "*Beta*" male, but is this really true? Here are my thoughts on this, based on my own experiences and knowledge.

Although the appearance and things of that nature are somewhat important, I think we can all agree upon one thing: Personality is still the most important factor and a selling point in every situation. No girl wants to date a guy with a bad personality who will mistreat her. Now, I'm not saying that all "*Alpha*" males are bad guys, but there are many girls out there that simply do not feel attracted to this type of males, instead they are looking for the complete opposite. Here's where we change the spotlight to the so-called "*Beta*" males.

If you feel like you're one of them and think this is what's stopping you from meeting or dating other females, I think you've come to the right place to be proven wrong. This E-Book will guide you, help you overcome your fear of approaching girls and reveal the hidden qualities that are buried deep under that thick layer of shyness which is preventing you from finding a beautiful significant other. Now I'm not saying that this is one of those "*guides*" that will automatically make you get infinite girls with "*one quick secret*" or a "*simple trick that science doesn't want you to know*", but I am sure that it will enlighten you just a bit so that you can get on the right track. I will give my best to share my own experiences with you, and teach you everything that I've learned in my past through the process of meeting and talking to females. You have to remember, change starts from within yourself if you cannot accept who you are and work on improving yourself as a person, nobody else will. Instead of trying to be something you're not, which will take a lot of your time for nothing, let's learn how to embrace what you already are and utilize it to your advantage. So without further ado, we're diving deeply into our first chapter.

Chapter 1

Are you a "Beta" male?

We hear how everyone is unique and special all the time. And, while that's true to some degree, guys can also fit into broad categories, based on certain traits.

While these terms are pretty questionable, it still might be possible to use the "*alpha*," "*beta*," or even "*omega*" to put men in different "*categories*". People invented these terms and use them to sort different types of males in the animal kingdom. Among humans, the alpha male is described as the courageous and attractive leader, the omega as the weird social vagabond, and the beta male is pretty often described as the passive guy who is many times frustrated with his lack of success women and relationships. Or, at least that's what everyone says about them.

But is what society says really true? I would personally have to disagree with this.

What Exactly does the Term *"Beta male"* Mean?

Beta males can often be characterized as someone that is thoughtful, knowledgeable and perceptive. Branded by many as a "*nerd*" or a "*geek*" while growing up, the adult beta is often a cautious, considerate, and most importantly a brilliant person that many women find attractive.

There are "*Alpha Males*" with lower levels of intelligence and abilities that sometimes tend to feel threatened by the "*Beta*" who's much more preferred by women in these modern times. Well, this doesn't sound so bad after all huh? Then why are you so worried about being a "*Beta*"? Is it because you heard that the girl you like only dates "*Alpha males*"? Is it because some random guy from your school years told you that you will never be an "*Alpha*" no matter how hard you try? If this is the case, you are already on the wrong path and you're wasting precious time of your beautiful life, worrying and stressing about things that should not affect you at all. Truth is, not everyone is born the same.

You should never ever feel bad about being a certain type of guy. We all have our qualities and talents, it's just that some of us have never looked deep inside them. Don't try to change yourself or do something stupid just so that you can impress that one girl that only likes dating "*Alphas*". You will most likely fail and make a fool out of you. Be yourself no matter what. Being "*Shy*" or "*Beta*" is not a curse. In fact, many people know how to utilize that as a perk. The main problem why shy guys have trouble with their confidence and overall with their personalities is because they think they're alone and that they are the only ones who suffer from this. They constantly look at other more successful males and compare themselves to them, and this will almost always result in even worse confidence. You need to understand that there are many other people feeling the same and that there is nothing wrong or weird about you. It's just how life plays out its roles and some people were born luckier than the others, but with enough practice and work, you can overcome anything. Instead of seeing your shyness as a flaw, you need to learn to take advantage of it. Being shy means you know how awkward you feel around other people, which means you can easily recognize the other shy person in the room, club or wherever you are. You need to understand that girls are not something that is unreachable and that you don't need superpowers just to get their attention. They are normal human beings, just like you, and they have the exact same feelings. They can also feel shy and embarrassed. In fact, most of the females that I met were very shy at first, but opened up their thoughts and emotions after a few simple lines of conversation. If you start a normal conversation I can guarantee you that they will engage in it and keep talking to you. Just remember to be nice and polite instead of trying to be a "*badass*" and act like you're unreachable.

Everybody falls for a nice personality, it's the most important factor when trying to leave a nice impression to someone. Conversations are a thing that you can practice and improve. They don't have to be in real life with a real person. You can practice by yourself at home or you can simply start talking to strangers on many different websites such as Omegle or Chatki. This way, nobody will know how you look like and what kind of a car or a job you have, it's just you and a bunch of virtual text messages, basically your playground for improvement. After you spend some time talking to a bunch of other people, you will slowly start to overcome your fear and anxiety and start realizing that you're just like everyone else. Remember to be yourself and be confident.

The most important thing is to utilize your "*Beta*" status to your advantage, and this takes us to our next chapter where you will learn exactly what this means and how to do it.

Chapter 2

Knowing your Strengths as a *"Beta"* Male

Being a *"Beta"* has its own strengths and advantages. Many females that were mistreated by the so-called *"Bad boys"* or *"Alphas"* will never think about going out with someone like that ever again. And this is where they take you into consideration. This is where you need to use this to your advantage. There are so many different things that you can offer them, that were never shown before by their previous *"Alpha"* partners. Many girls say that *"Alpha"* men sometimes treat them more like an accessory than a partner.

> *"They're great at faking an intense connection to lure you into their trap. They say everything you want to hear and can sweep a girl off her feet".*

But when it comes down to it, they talk the talk, but do they walk the walk?

They promise you the world, but do they deliver on that? No. Even so, so many of us keep hoping and waiting for it to come."

This is what kind of impression is left to a girl after dating an "*Alpha bad boy*". Does this sound like she had a good time? I'm pretty sure it does not. So when the time comes for her to choose another partner, do you think she will do the same mistake again? Of course not, she already learned her lesson, and now it is time for her to find a partner that will love her and care for her.

When a girl was asked what is it that she sees in a "*Beta*" guy that is so much more attractive than an "*Alpha*" guy, she said this:

"You can be vulnerable with them and fully open yourself, letting all of your feelings come out. If I showed vulnerability to my ex "Alpha" male boyfriend, he'd later use it to shame me and make fun of me in front of his friends just so he can look more "Manly"

and "Bad" in their eyes. He only cared about his reputation and maintaining his status. Now that I look back to it I find this so gross and I would never date a guy like that again. If I can't reveal vulnerability, if I can't show him who I really am, how can I forge the deeper connection needed for a long term relationship? My current "Beta" boyfriend knows my flaws, all of my weakness and fears. He has allowed me to be vulnerable, but has never used it as a weapon against me. The more we've revealed about ourselves, the deeper and stronger connection we forged. "Beta" boys are not afraid of emotion, nor of their own emotional side. "Beta" males are secure in themselves, they don't feel threatened and have no need for jealousy. "

I'm sure that your confidence rises just by reading some of these things. Being called a *"Beta"* wasn't so awful after all? Well, here is just a bit more music for your ears.

> *"The one thing that was truly killing me was that I had to ask for permission every*

single time that I wanted to spend time alone with my close friends. Believe it or not, it did not even matter if we're talking male or female here. Yes, you heard it correctly. Forget about even mentioning male friends or colleagues. "Alpha" males even get jealous of your girlfriends. Girl's nights out will not be worth it, for the interrogation that you will be getting the next morning. My "Alpha" boyfriends were all total control freaks. They isolate you. They want to control you. If another man even looks at you, it is your fault automatically, and you are probably already having an affair with him."

Now, the point of this example is not to bash on all the Alpha males, but to instead remind you that not every girl out there desires or even less, needs a guy like this. But if these types of guys are so bad and mistreat girls so much, why they still end up getting them in the first place, you ask yourself. Well, do you remember how many times you fell down when you were trying to learn how to walk? That's right. Life has its own ways of teaching us certain things. We're not here to change destiny, we are here to learn how to get the attention of females. So let's continue with some of the perks of having the "*Beta*" status.

Reasons Why Girls Like "Beta" Males

Quiet confidence is so much sexier than arrogance hiding insecurity

Many girls might think that "*Beta*" guys are boring. Yes, if you've dated an arrogant alpha male that made a drama out of every little thing, it will take a while to get used to the quiet confidence that these so-called "*Beta*" males have. They're not boring, you are just used to dating a jerk. Sorry but it's the truth.

> *"My husband's confidence might be of the quieter kind, but it's underpinned by a strength I've never seen in a man before. He is always here to lift me up and support me when things go wrong. In such a moment, my ex "Alpha male" boyfriend would be running miles away from the situation. I would never make the same mistake again on dating such a guy. To be honest I am even starting to question who is the real Alpha here."*

We need to respect women, not treat them like accessories. Show them your support when they need it, encourage them, lift them up and tell them they are beautiful. Be proud of their achievements and encourage them to do what they love most. If someone else compliments her, instead of trying to act "*Alpha*" by getting all angry and yelling, simply agree with him. She is your girl after all, right? You will look much sexier and confident in her eyes if you remain calm instead of making a drama. Real men don't make drama.

"*Beta*" males don't need a power struggle, or to be in control of everything.

> *"One minute they can be strong for you, the next you can be for them. That's okay. They don't fear to show you their weaker side. In fact, if you try to control them, rescue them or change them, they're more likely to walk away. They allow you to be yourself. They love you unconditionally and expect you to offer the same thing."*

This is something that is extremely important. I've heard many different stories of girls that complain about their abusive *"Alpha"* boyfriend asking them to change their looks, hairstyle, makeup or attitude, just so they can impress their friends. They don't let their girls be themselves, instead, they force them to be the person only they like them to be. No girl wants to be treated like this.

Why Smart Asian Females Tend to Almost Always Pick a *"Beta"* over The *"Alpha"* Male

While we're at it, I would like to mention a very interesting fact. Girls in Asian countries always tend to go for the so-called *"Betas"* instead of the *"Alpha Males"*. I'm not saying that this does not happen in other countries as well, but statistically, it is highest in Asian countries. Two known reasons for this are:

They are not shallow and don't judge people just by their visual appearances.

They are practical and responsible and want a partner with the same qualities.

Asian women tend to marry nice guys who are good providers, even when biologically they might be more attracted to guys that have the more "*Alpha*" look. This is simply because it is far more important in life to have someone who is responsible and productive, someone who will provide a good life and a bright future for the family.

At the end of the day, those males who are able to ensure existence for their families are the real "*Alphas*".

So now that we know many of the flaws that girls see in the "*Alpha males*", it is time to find someone to whom we can show that dating a "*Beta*" male is completely opposite of what people think it is. This takes us to our next chapter.

Chapter 3

Checking Your Reality Standards

Now that you have overcome your fear and anxiety of talking to other girls, it is time to look at the list of places where you can actually engage in a conversation with a female that you like. But first, you need to review your standards again and be very real with yourself. While I'm not saying that leagues exist and that some girls should be completely unreachable, you should be honest and ask yourself if you really want to approach that hot model at the bar while weighing 240lbs yourself and being completely out of shape. A simple way of doing a reality check is by simply asking yourself some questions on what your ideal girlfriend would look like. It should look something like this:

What is your ideal girlfriend like?

What qualities does she possess?

What are her interests?

What does she value the most?

How does she spend her time?

...

Now do the same for her physical attributes and looks.

Is she taller or shorter?

What kind of clothes does she usually wear?

What physical shape is she in?

Does she wear lots of makeup or prefers the "*natural look*"?

What kind of a hairstyle does she have?

...

Get as detailed as you can. The clearer you can imagine her in your mind, the better.

Also, you need to understand that even if your standards are down to earth and honest, there is a possibility that someone will just not like you and you might get rejected. There doesn't have to be anything wrong or bad about you, it's just that some people simply can't click with a certain person. I am pretty sure that you do not instantly desire every single girl that you saw in your life, there must be many that you simply dislike, not that you ever talked to them or anything it's just because their appearance is not that appealing to you. This is perfectly normal.

Ways and Options to Meet Other Girls

If you are a guy that does not have a lot of friends, or maybe you are just new and moved in the area just recently, you have many different places where you can go out and meet new people. A good and fun choice would be to visit the local clubs. Maybe take the time and learn some cool dance moves to impress the people around you. People that are good dancers are often very positive people and they almost instantly attract the attention of others. If you are a person that enjoys going to bars, you can search if there are any nearby and visit them, there are countless happy love stories of couples that randomly met at a bar while just trying to have a quick drink and go home. People are usually very talkative and friendly in such places, so you should have no trouble starting a talk with someone. Make sure you are polite, ask them how they're doing and focus on the conversation. Think of the times when you practiced with strangers on the internet. Try to always be funny and cheerful, people don't want any negativity when they are out in the bar just looking to have a good time. Try finding common interests and talk about those, if you see that you are both into reading books, for example, ask about their favorite book and other things on which you can both provide different opinions. Make sure to ask questions so that you are not the only one talking. If you see that the girl you're talking to is not very interested in your conversation, don't be weird and keep pushing it. Instead, simply leave. You need to understand that being rejected by a girl is totally normal and has happened to everyone. Even "*Alpha*" males often get rejected. Accept it and move on. Not everything goes the way we want it to.

If you still find it somewhat difficult to make the first talk and introduction in person, you can try some online dating applications or websites. This way, you can select countless interests and hobbies that you have, and you will be matched with women that share the exact same interest. Now you can straight talk about things you both love doing. Chances are if you are shy you can find someone who is also shy and wants to meet new people this way too. After a while, if you see that your conversations are deep and have a meaning, you should consider asking that person out on a dinner or a date. Remember that it is only awkward if you make it awkward. If you want to go out with a girl, the best thing you can do is let her know. Girls always appreciate confidence (not arrogance, just confidence). Don't mince words, don't babble on around the actual question, just ask her out. She'll either say yes or no, and if she does say no, that's totally fine. It doesn't have to be awkward, in fact, that's literally the least awkward way to do it. The more complicated you make it, the more awkward it is going to get if you get turned down. You'll either get a happy yes or maybe just a polite no, or rarely, a bitchy or sarcastic response. But, as we learned previously, everything that happens should be a lesson in life, do not let this put you down or ruin your motivation of trying again. Simply accept it and move on. What doesn't kill you makes you stronger after all, so go there and ask that girl out!

If she accepts, you can do some planning for the night that will guarantee you leave a good impression. Make sure you choose a fine place for the first meet. If you previously talked about different food tastes, surprise her by taking her to a place that matches the food she said she likes. Women love guys that remember small and not so important details from your conversations. By the time goes by you will forget that you ever had a problem doing this or that you ever felt awkward. Just enjoy the moment and be yourself.

Setting Up the Right Mindset

The main thing for meeting new people is actually exposing yourself to them. Oh really Sherlock? Yes, it sounds stupid but it is the truth. You can't sit the entire day at home and expect that new people will just come to your house and ask if you want to be their friend.

Shy people can often be more scared and anxious just by the thought of meeting someone new than the event itself. The thoughts and imaginations in our head about how the entire situation will turn out can frighten us more than what the actual reality, some people tend to imagine the worst case scenario in their mind and make a picture in their head that they will embarrass or make a fool out of themselves. This alone is enough to get the mental blockade which will even further prevent them to perform well when it comes time for the actual event.

If you manage to train your mind to always imagine a scenario where everything goes according to your plans and expectations, you will have no troubles when the time comes to meet that new person. Make sure that you always imagine the situation going smoothly and in your favor and let the positive thoughts about yourself flow freely.

This is proven to work because if you visualize the event positively your brain will experience a more familiar situation as opposed to if you constantly imagine a disaster.

The only way to grow in confidence is to face your fears. The more you let negative thoughts take over your mind, the more they start slowly taking control of your everyday life and social situations that you find yourself in. Challenge this thinking, not only by replacing negative thoughts with more positive ones, but also by confronting what you fear with action. Start going out more in an attempt to confront your shyness. Take baby steps initially and perhaps meet a friend on a one-to-one basis. Slowly start building up your social connections and involve yourself in activities that will allow you to meet new people with similar interests. Start visiting places, go to events and parties, get the best experience out of your life and everything else will come to its place. All of these activities will increase your social network. The more you have in common with the people around you, the easier it will be to interact and have conversations.

Sitting home and over thinking only leads to more anxiety. Like the legendary Bruce Lee once said: *"If you spend too much time thinking about a thing, you'll never get it done"*. And while we are at Bruce Lee, we've all seen that remarkable body of his. And what does this remind us of? That's right! Exercise. And what does exercise help us with? Literally everything! Which takes us right to our next chapter.

Chapter 4

The Art of Self-improvement

Having a Goal and a Plan

When it comes to self-improvement, there are many different things that each of us can do to become a better version of ourselves. This should not only be done to get a female's attention, but instead should become an everyday healthy habit. Each morning should be your perfect time and opportunity to do something better in your life. If you focus and dedicate on improving yourself, other people will notice this and start respecting you more. Your status and reputation will change in people's eyes and this further increases your chance of meeting someone new. You never know what life has prepared for you.

Make someone's day better and yours will be good as well. Tell your family members and friends that you love them and that you appreciate them being in your life.

We are what we believe we are, and we are capable of what we believe we are capable of. This is not just a random motivational quote, this is the truth that psychology has concluded in experiments throughout the last 20 years.

You control your mind, your destiny and your situation.

I hope you agree with what I'm saying, but just agreeing is not good enough. Just like deciding you believe in being healthy won't actually result in you being healthier or working out every day. Agreeing in a principle with that statement will usually get you nowhere.

Your goal should not be to change "*this, this or that*", your goal should be to get yourself to believe that you are the master of your mind. That takes weeks, months and often years of daily training. Nonetheless, when you finally master this, you will be able to make significant changes in your life with just a few thoughts. Master self-control and you can master everything else.

Focus on the reward, not the task. If you are trying to build a good looking and healthy body, think of all of the compliments you will be receiving and all the good you are doing for yourself, not the tough process and hard work that you have to go through.

Set plans and goals and slowly progress in any of them. Apply for that job that you want, date that person that you like, purchase that plane ticket, move into that city. Do all of the things that scare you or excite you. They are all so much worth it. Never be afraid to take risks and opportunities, even if you fail at something, you can always make a great and fun story out of it. And now from an unsuccessful attempt, you suddenly have one more interesting thing about yourself that you can tell on that date. Keep this mindset and always look on the bright side of life. Positivity is a key that unlocks many locked doors.

Rome wasn't built in a day, but they kept laying bricks every hour.

Dealing with Negative People in Your Life

There are people in the world who will be inspired by your efforts to improve, most people won't care, and some will **hate to see you improve**. I've never understood why someone would root against someone else. Some people just have a fixed mindset and think they will never change and others can't either.

We've all made mistakes and we all wish we were better. Invite these kinds of people to join you on the quest of self-improvement. If they don't want to come along, do your best to keep them from holding you back. When people become better, it makes the world better. We're all in this together. Constantly remind yourself to ignore the negativity.

Physical Transformation for increased Confidence

Some of the best things that you can do to yourself are to engage in some sport or get a gym membership. Exercise not only helps you get physically fit, healthy and good looking, but it also reduces stress level and helps with anxiety. People that regularly train and live a healthy and happy life shine with positive energy and people love being around them.

"Steve is really confident lately, he looks pretty good as well, perhaps he started working out? How about I go ahead and ask him?" Do you want this to be the thought that goes through that cute girl's head that's checking you out from across your work desk? If the answer is yes, you better start self-improvement today. You won't believe how such small changes to your life might show you the way to something great.

Regular physical activity produces changes in the parts of the brain that regulate stress and anxiety. It also increases brain sensitivity for the hormones serotonin and norepinephrine, which relieve feelings of depression. On top of that, it increases the production of endorphins, which are known to help produce positive feelings. All of this will have a very positive impact on your confidence.

Plus, after all the gym is one more place where you can meet new friends, workout buddies and even girls, just do not be that guy that approaches girls in the middle of their sets. A great advice if you want to approach a girl at the gym is to possibly wait for her to finish her workout, or if you really want to do it, do it after she is done with her set and has her headphones taken off, not while she's in the middle of lifting.

Many shy guys think that going to the gym would be awkward and that they will be made fun of, but this is almost never the case. I am going to the gym for a long time and never have I seen someone make fun out of a new person, instead, I've witnessed more experienced lifters to actually go and give them friendly advice. Many friendships start from just a simple quick talk. So take a deep breath, pack your gym bag and start your fitness journey. This will develop a strong character and discipline, you will learn to love your body and respect yourself even more. There is no time for excuses, there are people out there that want to see the new and improved version of yourself.

Visual Appearance and Confidence Levels

While working out and hitting the gym regularly will directly impact your visual appearance, there are many other different things that you can do that will make you feel more confident. Remember, looks are not the most important thing, but having that haircut that you always wanted or that cool shirt that you were checking out yesterday sure help you to some point..

You don't need to spend tons of money to buy clothes from expensive brands hoping you will look better, simply wear clothes that make you feel comfortable and let you be yourself. It is better to wear a 10$ shirt that you are comfortable in than a 400$ that will make you sweat and itch and doesn't match your tone color at all.

Chapter 5

Matching Lifestyles and Compatibility in a Relationship

I deeply believe that one of the biggest and most important reasons why friendships and relationships are created and last long times are matching lifestyles and common interests. One of the first things that people ask each other after meeting up for the first time is about their hobbies and what they love doing in their free time. If you are into something, video games, for example, it will be much better and easier at the same time to find a girl that is into gaming as well. If you meet a female with the same interests, you already have half of the way paved for you. You have the necessary topic, all you have to do is start a conversation about it. Ask her if she wants to play that video game together, ask if she plays any other games besides the one you just talked about, maybe show her some other games that are fun but she doesn't know of yet.

If you are both into music, you can exchange different group names and types of music. Play some instrument together or go to a music show. Maybe take her to a music shop and buy her a gift, a simple vinyl from her favorite band will mean a lot to her. Sentimental things are what matter the most. Successful and long relationships are based on so little yet very important details.

Couples that do the same hobbies and activities together, usually stay together forever. There are countless stories about couples that met on a video game and got married. You never know who you are going to meet. Life offers beautiful things to us every day, we just need to recognize and grab them.

Signs that You and Your Partner are Compatible

There is no such thing as two people that match perfectly by nature. It is absolutely normal for you to feel difficult sometimes, especially when you find a number of big differences between you and your partner. But, this does not mean that you are not compatible with your partner.

There are also a number of very important factors which determine how long your relationship can last. Below, I will mention some of the signs that can help you see if you and your partner are a matching couple.

1. You don't question the love in your relationship.

You know you love your partner, and you know they love you and there is not a gram of doubt in your mind about any of these things. You are secure and happy in your relationship, and even if you are a worried or anxious person by nature, you never question how your partner feels about you. This is one of the most important signs that you have a healthy and good relationship

2. You know things about each other no-one else does.

As weird as it may sound, sharing embarrassing stories and intimate details of your life with your partner will let them know that you really trust them and that exposing your vulnerable side to them is not a problem for you. Intimacy and trust are the most important elements of a relationship, so make sure you let your partner know that you possess both of those. If you open up with such details, they will be happy to share their secrets with you as well. You might find something new about each other that might make you even closer than you already are.

3. You don't want to change them.

You have total respect for your partner and you love them just the way they are, even with some of their flaws. Nobody's perfect and we all know this very well. Maybe your partner sometimes talks very loudly or wears something that doesn't match him at all but you still love and appreciate them for who they are.

4. You enjoy spending time apart.

When you are into a relationship, especially a new one, there is a period called the "*honeymoon*" and this is where you feel basically un-attachable from your partner and living without them seems very hard and almost impossible for you. Although this is a good thing, you still need to understand that sometimes spending time apart is very important. This will not make you both get used to living without each other, so don't worry about that. In fact, it will make you miss each other even more and value each other's presence when you finally get back together.

5. You share common interests.

While it is very important to have your own hobbies and interests that you enjoy spending time on, couples that share the love for the same activities usually push each other towards success in all of those fields. For example, if you both love bodybuilding you will give each other motivation when you sometimes feel down and lack the will to hit the gym. If you love video games you can both help each other in different areas to become better at what you're doing.

6. You fight with each other.

If you disagree with your partner on something, they should listen to what you have to say and you should also listen to their opinion on it. Even if you can't manage to agree on something after countless conversations about it, it is still perfectly fine. One disagreement will not change anything that you feel for each other. Also, opposite opinions sometimes attract even more. At the end of the day, you will just laugh it off and probably end up cuddling.

7. You want to work out serious problems.

Often big issues can be raised in long term relationships, including financial situations, different religions or beliefs or where you both live. Sometimes even some family members can cause problems and unnecessary drama, but you should not let this ruin your relationship. It is very important to talk about big problems and solve them as normal and civilized human beings. Don't be stubborn, if your partner is right about something you should accept their opinion.

Chapter 6

Improving the Quality of Your Relationship

If you are already in a relationship but for some reason, you are having troubles or you just want to improve the overall quality, I have some tips and experiences that I learned from my previous long term relationships.

Listening to your Partner

This might sound like a pretty obvious thing for me to state, but when you really allow yourself to ask questions and listen what your partner has to say, it will lead to more quality conversations and overall better communication between you two. This is always a key factor in many relationships, so take this advice carefully.

Be helpful to each other

Moral support is great, but sometimes you need to help each other with chores and other necessary, if banal, activities such as cooking, cleaning, washing the dishes or feeding the pets. Not helping in such things while living together can create a lot of unwanted tension, and always doing them can create unfair expectations, so act as a team of equals. Split them equally and do them equally. Balance is key for everything.

Allow things to be what they are

Sometimes bad days and bad moods happen. It's just how life goes. Don't go crazy trying to make everything better. Just be supportive and loving, because just being there at the end of a bad day can make it a lot better for both of you.

Be an open book. Don't keep any secrets that shouldn't be kept away

They can either deal with it or they can't, but if you can't be your most honest self with your partner, it will come out to the surface eventually and in a very bad way. In a relationship, uncovering a secret **about your partner but not from your partner** is one of the most frustrating things that might lead to big trust issues and a possible break-up.

Compliment on small things and do them very often

You're there to make each other feel like you are the best version of your selves, so let the positive thoughts flow freely. If you like the outfit of your partner, say it. Don't keep these things in secret. If you like the way their hair is today, let them know. Things like this increase their confidence and make your relationship much better.

Establish good connections with your partner's friends and family

Go out and spend some time with both of your friends and family. This is the stuff that makes the world a better place. Introduce her to your friends and vice versa. Throw in a double date from time to time, those things are fun and make your relationship bond stronger. Maybe call a couple of your or his/her friends and have a sleepover or go to the movies together. Small group activities build the biggest connections and chemistry.

Be considerate and talk about your problems

If you had a bad day, it is not your partner's fault. Don't take out all the anger that your boss caused inside you on the people that love you and care about you. If you are not in the mood to talk or do anything that day, just say it and they will understand. Trying to hide it and just being passive aggressive will lead to an argument and give a false impression to your partner that they're doing something wrong even when they're just trying to figure out why you are in a bad mood. If you simply talk about it you will both just end up laughing it out and everything will go back to normal.

Let the bad things that happened go, bury them deep in the past and keep looking forward

Don't hold onto things that your significant other said or did half a year ago. Don't bring this up each time you guys get into an argument. Do yourself and everyone a favor and let it go. If you start bringing things up that happened in the past each time you argue, your partner will start seeing it like the only way to deal with an argument and he/she will start doing it too. This will trigger a chain reaction of unwanted events that can really ruin your relationship. **Learn to forgive and you will be forgiven.**

Don't interrupt when he/she is talking

Even if you feel bored or uninterested from what your significant other is saying, don't interrupt. Being able to listen to each other even when things are not that appealing or fun to you is one of the most important things in a relationship. Maybe sometimes you're saying something boring and dull as well, but you don't want to be interrupted, do you?

Take happiness into your own hands

Love is everything, but we must not wait for our entire lives on someone to love us so that we can be happy and satisfied. **The only person that can love you the most is you**, and if you want to be loved by others you have to truly live by these words. The more you work on yourself to become a better person, the more love you will be getting from everyone around you.

Define what "*love*" really means to you

While "*I love you*" is an extraordinary thing to say, and an equally wonderful thing to hear, it means something different to each person. **Tell each other what you mean when you say these words. It could mean a lot of things from "*I would do anything for you*" to "*I trust you completely*".**

Ask for a simple explanation.

If you sometimes don't really understand what your partner is trying to tell you, ask for a simple explanation. Use an open phrase like "*What did you exactly mean to say when you said that thing last night?*" This is so much better than just going on the offensive side instantly and causing an unwanted argument that might lead to some bad things later on in the relationship.

Don't be a control freak just so you can show her "*who is the male of the house*".

A relationship is not a battle of who will control the other person more, it's just two people who are choosing to be together and love each other for a long time, so you really must not treat your partner like they are some kind of a wild animal and your mission is to tame it. If you really love and care about your partner you need to set them out of the cage. Let them do what they love doing and they will do the same for you. Think of it like a bird in a cage, if you love the bird would you trap it in a cage or let it fly freely and enjoy the beauty of free and borderless life?

Take your time and learn to breathe.

Before you say something that you do not mean, take a breath and ask yourself if that's really the way you want to move forward. Chances are, taking a second out will help you recalibrate and think of a more constructive way of handling the current problem or situation that you are facing. There are countless relationships that are ruined by going into raging outbursts and saying things that might leave a deep scar on your partner's feelings.

Do not listen to what others say.

Okay, I cannot stress how important this one is. If you feel like you've chosen the right partner for you and if you see that everything is going the way it should and you are both happy having each other, there is absolutely no need to listen to what others have to say about you being together with them. Many times friends or even other not so close but very jealous people, can ruin relationships that would usually last forever by telling those people lies and making up fake stories about something that never happened, just so they can split up. If there is anything that you want to know about, simply ask your partner instead of asking your friends what they think. This way you will get the most honest and accurate answer, and you will most likely save your relationship.

Chapter 7

Dealing with Anxiety and Rejection

One of the main problems why people are afraid to attempt different things in life is the possibility to fail. People take failure as something that should put you down forever and destroy your will to try again, but this is very wrong. Every failure that happens in life should be just another lesson that motivates us, even more, to strive for success and get that thing done no matter how hard you have to try. Failure and pain are the best teachers in life.

This applies to dating and love life as well.

I've literally never heard of a guy that has one hundred success percentage with picking up other girls. Even the most famous and handsome guys, share at least one story of a girl that rejected them when they asked her out.

You need to understand that this is completely normal and that will happen to you at least once or even many times, but should not stop you from trying to find your perfect match.

We've all been rejected before, keep your head up.

Rejection is probably the biggest fear factor when it comes to dating. It unlocks a place from where our worst fears about simply not being good enough come out. The unfortunate fact is that it is a common part of the dating process and if you learn how to cope with it, the entire journey will be much more enjoyable for you.

Don't take these kinds of situations straight to your heart

When someone rejects you, it might be difficult at first to not take it personally and blame yourself. There is a chance that if you have been talking online, or only had a few dates, you both simply did not find what you were looking for. This does not mean that the problem is in you. Everyone has a special recipe for what defines their "*perfect partner*". This is almost always formed by our past experiences, our expectations for the future, biological factors and personal preferences. It very rare that anyone ever finds the type of partner that matches all these standards and when the feeling is the exact same from the other side, it's a cause for celebration. This is one of the main reasons why love is so appreciated, sought after and can seem like it is pretty difficult to find.

When someone rejects you it's because you aren't the right match for their personality, not because there's anything wrong with you. It doesn't mean that you won't be perfect for someone else.

Let them go if that's how it is supposed to be

When you find someone that you think has the potential to be your "*perfect partner*" you will most likely do anything in your power to keep them close to you, but if you see that things are simply not working out the way they should, it is much better for your own good to let them go gracefully. Don't try to force things that were never meant to happen. You will only get more hurt and disappointed when life finally separates you in its own way. Forced relationships always fail because of inequality, you deserve someone that will feel the exact same way that you feel for them, so let go while it's still time. You will feel much better and look better in the eyes of the person that you're splitting with. No matter how much it hurts or we hate doing it, sometimes letting go of someone is just the correct thing to do.

Build a *"thick and tough skin"*

One of the best ways to deal with rejection is to simply feel good about yourself. If you're feeling comfortable in your own skin, confident when you go on dates, certain in your skills and qualities, then rejection will be easily accepted as part of not just dating but everyday life and only viewed as a valuable lesson, nothing more. It is sometimes a bit harder to let go when you already get attached to someone and they suddenly change their mind and decide they don't want to be with you anymore, so knowing when to step away is very important. It can be a bit painful at first yes, but you must not let it ruin your quest for finding the love you deserve.

In a strange way, being rejected while trying to find the right person can be of great help with your future relationships. Knowing you can handle it and building your resilience can mean that when you do finally meet your special person you will be stronger and more confident than you would've been otherwise.

When the "*tables turn*" and now you're the one rejecting

Sometimes you'll be the one doing the rejecting and this can be just as hard as being rejected. You might have dates that fall for you completely, but you just don't get the same feeling about them. This can be especially difficult if you're feeling empathy to other people's feelings but it is really important that you are very clear and sure the decision that you're making.

If you feel someone is not the right match for you, instead of giving them all the false hope that will later just hurt them a lot, simply tell them the truth. Be honest and don't make excuses, lie or try and sugar coat it in compliments because they might take that as a sign that they should keep on trying.

By giving them a simple and honest "*Thanks but I don't think that me and you will click* together" or" *Hey, it's nothing personal, I just feel like you are not the one for me*" you acknowledge them to fully turn their effort and attention to other dates rather than wasting their time on something that will just not work out the way it should.

It might sound like a good idea to try and not hurt that someone who is into you rather than risk upsetting them or making them cry, but in the long run this is really unfair for the other person and will almost end with "*You should've just told me from the start instead of lying*". You need to let them go so that you open that door in your life for the special person to come in when the time is right. Treat people the way that you want to be treated.

Chapter 8

The infamous *"Friend Zone"*

Finally, what we've all been waiting for. The solution for this notorious confidence breaker of men.

We have all heard about it or even visited this dark place at least once before in our lives. The nightmare of every guy on this world. Often a reason why hearts are broken and friendships torn apart ended in tears. The only thing that hurts more than a bullet shot right through your chest. The infamous *"Friend Zone"*.

How you are supposed to survive this living hell, you ask yourself. "*What did I ever do to deserve to be stuck here*" is a very common phrase that you can hear when you look down into the depths of this place. How do you motivate a friend to be "*more than just friends?*" How do you move forward from "*just friends*" to girlfriend, partner or a lover? The ultimate question follows. How does one trapped warrior escape the friend zone?

I am sure that this is one of the most frequently asked questions on the internet. Many fallen warriors seeking advice on how to heal their wounds and get back up on their feet again. Some manage to do it, some get stuck there for a very long time. I have advice and tips for both kinds.

So, for being able to escape the friend zone, you need to learn and understand what exactly a "*friend zone*" means. This term is used to describe a situation where one person in a friendship starts developing stronger feelings for the other person and wants to take it to the next level and upgrade the status of "*friends*" to "*more than just friends*". Often, the other person is not aware of the friend's desires and plans and is quite satisfied with the just friendship situation. Because of this, the person is "*trapped*" in the so-called "*friend zone*" and is unable to change their status from a "*friend*" to a" *partner*".

Being stuck in such a place can be pretty frustrating. Sometimes this frustration is sexually-motivated, which means that the "*trapped*" person wants a physical relationship with the other. Another situation would be when the friends are already in a sexual relationship, but there is a motivation to turn this from a "*friends with benefits relationship*" to a "*dedicated girlfriend or boyfriend relationship*". In other cases, both motivations might be the cause. Anyway, wanting more than you are getting at the moment is a pretty tough situation. The "*friend zone*" is a very rough place to find yourself in.

Why Does *"The Friend Zone"* Happen?

Before I am able to guide you on how to get out of this place, we first need to review and discuss why people end up being there. Almost every relationship is some kind of social trade. This means that people set up "*give-and-take terms*" in order to get what they want from the other person and give what they are willing and able to give.

When someone gets stuck in the friend zone it means that they are into a "*give and take*" friendship that is not equal and only satisfies the needs of one of the two people involved in it. That person is receiving everything that he or she desires, but the person stuck in the friend zone is simply left empty-handed. The truth is, the friend-zoned person sold himself short or so-called "*played himself*". They gave their "*friend*" everything, without making sure they got all the things that they wanted in return.

Let me provide some examples to help you understand what I'm trying to say to all of you reading this right now.

Matt and Mia are friends. As "*friends*", Matt pretty much does everything for Mia. He takes her good places to eat, buys her gifts, listens to all she has to say and helps her when she needs it the most. Matt wants to be Mia's boyfriend. Mia though, isn't interested because she is having all of her "*boyfriend*" needs provided by Matt, without having to provide his. She can be free and do whatever she wants, and still have all of Matt's effort. That is why Matt is stuck in the friend zone.

Another example just like this one but with the roles switched up would look something like this.

Angela and Peter are *"friends with benefits"*. They meet and spend some time together. Angela, however, wants to be in a relationship with Peter, but he is happy to just hook up. He is being sexually fulfilled, without having to satisfy Angela's needs. This type of exchange is not in Angela's favor and she has nothing left to trade with, which means that she is now stuck in the friend zone. Yes, girls are stuck in the friend zone too, do not be amazed by this, it actually happens pretty often.

So now that we've learned what this term means, let's look at the ways and options of someone who's trying to overcome and escape the friend zone.

How to Escape the Friend Zone

The *"Being less interested and/or available"* method.

The relationship is already unfair and not balanced because you value it more than the other person. Take a step back and reconsider your trading skills. Being *"needy"* is no way to get what you want or negotiate. People who are desperate, very often end up with what other people give them, not what they really wish or deserve to have. So, be less interested in things that are simply not in your favor and prepare to walk away if you don't get the relationship you want. This may sound harsh and hard to do at first, but trust me, it works and makes the other person question their decisions. At the end of the day, even if you end up losing the person, it will just serve you as a useful experience for your other upcoming scenarios. Those who are more willing to walk away are able to control the tide.

Another interesting method that is also proven to work, is spending some time away from your "*friend*" and doing less for them. If they truly appreciate you and value your presence, then your absence will make them miss you and want you more. This is the principle of "*Scarcity*" – where people value something more when it is rare or taken away from them.

When you are no longer around so much or doing the favors that they need, I am pretty sure that they are going to feel the loss. This will almost always increase their desire for you and empower their will to bring you back in their lives. If this does not work, then they are just "*not that into you*" and don't value you a lot as a person. If this is the case, simply go and find yourself another person. You were not going to make it work with the previous one anyway, so you just saved yourself a lot of time and dodged many stressful situations.

Stand Up for Yourself and Create a Bit of Competition

Go out and make some other "*friends*" of the opposite sex. Expand your social network. Then, talk about these new friends with the "*friend*" that you really desire. Competition and a little jealousy are just another great way of making them develop their feelings for you. People value more what they think they might lose or "*can't have*". If you are getting "*busy*" with other people, you might just find your friend a bit more interested and glad for your time and attention. If you don't see any "*jealousy*" though, then they might not want to be "*more than friends*". In that case, set your focus on finding someone new. I'm pretty sure you've heard the story about Eve and the "*forbidden fruit*". Well, I want you to do exactly the same, I want you to be a "*forbidden fruit*". People always strongly desire the things that are forbidden to them or that they cannot get very easily.

Involve them into investing a bit themselves in the current relationship

Ask your friend to do things for you. Unlike many things, people like you more when they are the ones doing favors for you, rather than when you do the favor for them. This is called the Ben Franklin Effect. The more they invest in the relationship, the more you will mean to them. So, stop only doing favors and instead, start asking for them. Get them to give you a ride somewhere, study something with you, lead you money, etc. Even asking them to get you a drink from the fridge has an impact! Just make sure you know the borderlines of being rude and asking for a normal favor in a polite way. Do not try to boss them around because this will only make you look like a jerk and ruin your reputation in their eyes.

Let them know that you appreciate what they are doing for you and that it means a lot

Don't forget to be grateful and reward your partner when they are kind and nice to you. After they do a favor to you, remember to always do something nice for them as well. Being warmhearted and kind when they do what you like, motivates them, even more, to continue doing these things for you. Also, ignoring them when they act inappropriately will help to reduce the bad and unwanted behaviors. Always remember to build an environment of mutual gratitude.

Doing the things mentioned above will balance the situation in your current relationship. It will highlight how truly important and irreplaceable you are to them. Most importantly, it will raise your status and reputation in their eyes.

From those first steps, it is a matter of changing the actual relationship, either by asking the question directly or indirectly. Maybe you would like to indirectly ask them out on a real date. Maybe you would prefer the face to face method. Or simply a conversation is more like your way of dealing with situations. In any case, find a way to either directly or indirectly ask for what you want, and you will be much more likely to get it. That is, unless they already find you so attractive now that they ask you first!

If you decide to ask, just make sure to use good body language yourself, look and act your best too. I believe that every single one of you reading this right now, has the required courage and charm needed to win a soul relieving "*yes*" from your "*friend*". You have everything that is required, make it happen.

Chapter 9

How to be Attractive without Trying Hard

Sometimes, life can be easier for people who are more physically attractive, in other words, it provides them a slight advantage or a head start in some aspects of life, including dating. How can you show your great personality to someone if they don't want to talk to you because you look and smell bad?

When someone sees you for the first time, the very first thing he notices is your physical appearance. Everyone knows that it's what's inside that matters, but they can't see what's inside until they get to know you.

But if you appeal unlikeable to them because of the clothes you're wearing or your hair and facial hair, they might not even want to talk to you. There are certain things that you can do in order to appear more attractive to others, and you don't necessarily have to even try that hard, a better word I would use is "*adapting*" to certain changes.

You should not be saving on important things like haircuts, shoes or something that will make you smell nice. Of all the things that you spend money on, when it comes to being more presentable and attractive to the world, one of the most important are those three. They always get noticed first and leave an impression based on how "*on point*" they are. If you look good and smell even better, you will feel great and confident about yourself. So if you can afford quality pieces of the above-mentioned items, go for it.

Take care of your body.

This doesn't mean you need to become a body-builder or marathon runner. Take care of your body by embracing a healthier lifestyle. Start by making basic every day healthy decisions, eat more fruits and vegetables, do a couple of pull-ups or maybe ride your bike. A healthy body is often times considered an attractive trait. Plus, as I mentioned in the previous chapters, you should be doing this for your own good, not for impressing others, but you will look much brighter and happier in other people's eyes if you take care of yourself.

Make better eye contact.

It's always better when someone is talking to you to look him in the eyes. When talking to the girl you like make better eye contact. It's one of the fastest way to display strong confidence, and confidence is sexy. You don't have to stare at her eyes all the time, but when you're telling her something important you should always give your best to maintain that eye contact.

Sleep well.

Get your daily dose of good sleep. Sleep deprived people always look less attractive and very unhealthy. That's why getting a good night sleep is one of the best things you can do to appear more energetic and fresh. Getting up to 8 hours of sleep each night will fight off red eyes, and other symptoms of sleep deprivation. You will be able to focus more on your conversations and everything in your surroundings. A good tip that is backed by science as well as to sleep in a dark room that's below average temperature. This helps the body rest and recover fully.

Smile more.

This one is so simple yet so important. When you smile you appear more approachable and friendlier. A smile makes you attractive, and if you smile at people they will smile back at you. Many people underestimate the power of one simple look in the eyes and a bright smile. Sometimes this alone can get you a new friend or a partner. You never know, so smile some more.

Dress nicely.

It's always important to wear nice clothes that fit you well and flatter your figure. The fastest way to appear attractive to someone is through your clothes. When it comes to style, wear whatever makes you feel sexy and good. Now, I've mentioned before that this is only optional and not the most important factor, but it is still a factor. Sadly, in the society that we live today, people will judge you a lot by how you look. Your clothes absolutely don't need to be expensive or some famous brand, just wear something nice and bright that matches your personality.

Conclusion

We live in a world where everyone is becoming soft, maybe not in a physical way, but in a moral way and in a mindset perspective. Most people decide to run away when faced with a problem, because they lack the mindset and mentality to deal with the given problem or situation, instead of facing that problem head-on. Problems are meant to be solved, and just like any problem if you think being a "*beta male*" is a " *problem*", then there is always a solution to that problem. People see you as a mediocre person who lacks charisma and physicality, confidence and success. You are regarded as a careful man, who avoids risks and tends to avoid the problems.

But in the modern day world, not all girls like the strong athletic macho guy who talks loudly and hits the gym to hide his insecurities. Yeah sure they talk the talk, but do they walk the walk? They promise you the world, but do they deliver it?

Being a "*beta*" means you are emotionally available to your partner, you don't want to lose her, you keep showing up in from of her and you tell her "*I'm here for you*". They trust you and you trust them, you won't take advantage of her trust, you won't take advantage of her if she feels vulnerable, you talk more and more and you reveal more and more about yourself to her and she loves that. Quiet confidence is so much sexier than arrogance hiding insecurity. Sure your confidence might be of the quieter kind, but you have the strength that no woman has seen in an "*alpha*" before. You possess something far sexier, you have the power and strength to be strong for your partner, to lift them and support them. You're nice, sweet and you treat your partner with respect, something she might not always get with an "*alpha*", you celebrate her success without being jealous at her accomplishments. You're not a person who will get into a power struggle with your partner, you don't fear showing your weaker side, you don't want to change her and you love her unconditionally, expecting the same in return.

With all this said, the main problem still persists, you are still running away from your problems. You can't run away from a problem in a relationship, meeting it head-on is the right way. Don't be scared to give your opinion to your partner, if she loves you back she will listen to you. Don't let her step on you and say to yourself "*that's fine*", don't let her take advantage of your emotions and good behavior. As much as those things are "*good*", they can be very, very "*bad*" if you end up with the wrong person. Here is where your mindset comes along. You finding the strength to say enough is enough if someone treats you like that, taking advantage of all those good traits. No matter how insecure you feel about yourself, you can't be treated like that. There will always be more fish in the sea, she not the first (probably) nor the last.

Thank you for reading " The Beta Male Dating Guide".

*If you enjoyed this book and found this book helpful, please consider leaving a review, **even if it's only a few lines; it would make all the difference and would be very much appreciated. Thank you!***

Ben Romero

www.ingramcontent.com/pod-product-compliance
Lightning Source LLC
Chambersburg PA
CBHW060411080526
44583CB00012B/528